Sermon Outlines
— ON —
The Book of Ephesians

David Graves

BEACON SERMON OUTLINE SERIES

Sermon Outlines
on
The Book of Ephesians

David Graves

Beacon Hill Press of Kansas City
Kansas City, Missouri

Copyright 2003
by Beacon Hill Press of Kansas City

ISBN 083-412-0364

Printed in the
United States of America

Cover Design: Paul Franitza

All Scripture quotations not otherwise designated are from the *Holy Bible, New International Version*® (NIV®). Copyright © 1973, 1978, 1984 by International Bible Society. Used by permission of Zondervan Publishing House. All rights reserved.

10 9 8 7 6 5 4 3 2 1

Contents

1. Spiritual Riches (1:3-14) — 7
2. A Sense of Destiny (1:3-6) — 9
3. Looking in Two Directions (1:3-14) — 11
4. The Power of the Resurrection (1:15-23) — 13
5. Paul's Prayer for Enlightenment (1:15-23) — 15
6. Our Authority in Christ (1:18—2:7) — 17
7. Taking Off Your Graveclothes (2:1-10) — 20
8. God's Workmanship (2:10) — 23
9. Grace—Past, Present, Future (2:11-22) — 25
10. A Mystery Revealed (3:1-13) — 27
11. Paul's Prayer for Enablement (3:1, 14-21) — 29
12. Living a Worthy Life (4:1-16) — 31
13. Off with the Old; On with the New! (4:17-32) — 34
14. Directives for the New Life (4:25—5:2) — 36
15. Imitating Our Father (5:1-17) — 38
16. Imitators of God (5:1-2) — 40
17. Always Giving Thanks (5:15-20) — 42
18. Life Can Be Gloriously Full (5:15-20) — 44
19. The Control of the Spirit (5:18) — 46
20. Life in the Spirit (5:18) — 48
21. Guidelines for Spirit-Filled Homes—Part 1 (5:18-33) — 50
22. Guidelines for Spirit-Filled Homes—Part 2 (5:18-33) — 52
23. Guidelines for Spirit-Filled Homes—Part 3 (6:1-4) — 54
24. Is There Hope for the Family? (5:33) — 56
25. Ready for Battle—Part 1 (6:10-24) — 58
26. Ready for Battle—Part 2 (6:10-24) — 61
27. Our Advantage in Battle—Prayer (6:10-24) — 63

Spiritual Riches

Ephesians 1:3-14

Introduction
She had gone down in history as "America's Greatest Miser," yet when she died in 1916, "Hetty" Green left an estate valued at over $100 million. She ate cold oatmeal, because it cost too much to heat it. Her son had to suffer a leg amputation, because she delayed so long looking for a free medical clinic. She was wealthy, yet she chose to live like a pauper. She hastened her own death by refusing to buy skimmed milk, because it cost more than regular milk. Eccentric, certainly! Crazy! Perhaps? Yet I am afraid that "Hetty" Green is an illustration of far too many Christian believers today. They have limitless spiritual wealth at their disposal, yet they live like spiritual paupers. The apostle Paul in his letter to the Ephesians wants believers to know that Jesus made it possible for all Christians to share in His spiritual riches. In verses 8-14 Paul informs us just how rich we really are in one long sentence.

- I. **Riches from Our Father (vv. 3-6)**
    - A. He chose us (v. 4).
        1. Paul never thought of himself as having chosen to do God's work.
        2. He always thought of God as having chosen him.
        3. John 15:16
        4. This is a wonder that God chose us to be His people and to bless us with heavenly riches.
        5. He chose us for a purpose.
            - *a.* To be holy (Rom. 12:1-2; 2 Tim. 1:9; 1 Pet. 1:15-16; 2:9; 2 Pet. 3:11).
            - *b.* To be blameless (Eph. 5:27; Phil. 2:15).
    - B. He has predestined us to be His children (v. 5).
        1. We become His children through adoption.
            - *a.* John 1:12
            - *b.* Gal. 4:1-7
        2. We become His children through acceptance.

　　　　a. There is an ancient Roman custom. Every newborn baby was brought before the father of the family. If the father picked up the baby, it was accepted into the family. However, if the father turned his back and walked away, the baby was left to die.
　　　　b. Our Heavenly Father accepts as His children all who repent of their sins and adopts them into His family.
　　　　c. He makes them holy and blameless through His Spirit.

II. Riches Through Jesus (vv. 7-12)
　　A. He has redeemed us (v. 7).
　　B. He has forgiven us (v. 7).
　　C. He has made known to us His will (v. 9).
　　D. He has made us His praise (v. 12).

III. Riches from the Holy Spirit (vv. 13-14)
　　A. He has given us a seal (v. 13).
　　　　1. A seal speaks of a finished transaction.
　　　　2. A seal speaks of ownership.
　　　　3. A seal speaks of security and protection.
　　　　4. A seal speaks of authenticity.
　　B. He has given us a deposit, His Holy Spirit (v. 14).

Conclusion

　　True riches do not come from investments in the stock market, collectibles, houses, property, or retirement accounts. True riches come from God. The reason God has given us His riches is for the praise of His glory (vv. 5, 12, and 14). God's purpose in saving us is that we may glorify Him. We don't deserve these spiritual riches; we receive them by grace through faith. There is no need to live in spiritual poverty when all of God's wealth is at our disposal. By faith we can claim God's promises and draw upon His limitless wealth to meet every need we may face.

A Sense of Destiny

Ephesians 1:3-6

Introduction
Some time ago there was a *Peanuts* cartoon in which Lucy is in the outfield playing a baseball game. Of course, Charlie Brown is on the pitcher's mound. Lucy calls out to him, "Hey, manager! Ask your catcher if he still loves me!" Charlie Brown interrupts his pitching and says to the catcher, "She wants to know if you still love her." In the next frame Charlie turns and yells to Lucy, "He says no!" Then Lucy wants to know why not. Charlie relays the information to Lucy again: "He says there are so many reasons he cannot remember them all." This upsets Lucy and she responds, "Really? That's very depressing." Finally, Charlie Brown, exasperated, cries out, "Do you mind if we get on with the game?" Lucy responds, "Game? What game?" "The baseball game!" shouts Charlie Brown, to which Lucy responds, "Oh, that's right. I was wondering why I was standing out here."

In the game of life it is good for us to pause at strategic points to ask ourselves why we are "standing out here." What is our purpose? Why are we here?

I. A Sense of Destiny (v. 5)
   A. Some people have a very strong sense of destiny.
   B. There are some people who believe that God has a plan for their lives, and they seek to live out that plan.
   C. They trust God with their lives.

II. A Sense of Destiny Gives Birth to a Determination (v. 4)
   A. People who have a sense of destiny accomplish more than those who do not have a sense of destiny.
   B. If you believe God is at work in your life and has a plan for your life, you will probably accomplish more than if you do not believe it.
   C. If you believe that God has a purpose for your life, you are more apt to look for ways to turn obstacles into opportunities.

III. A Sense of Destiny Gives Birth to a Determination That Develops a Strong Faith
A. Good things and bad things happen to everyone. The question is, How do you interpret those things?
B. If we interpret a setback as momentary, a fluke, only a pebble and not an insurmountable boulder, then we are more apt to seek to turn life's lemons into lemonade.
C. Faith contends that in the sum total of things, if we trust in God, life will work out according to His plans.

Conclusion
As we consider our destiny in relation to God, let us choose to believe:
1. God has predestined us to be adopted as His children through Jesus Christ, in accordance with His pleasure and will.
2. All things will work together for good for those who love God.
3. Though we can see only the tangled, confused underside of life, God is busy weaving a beautiful pattern that will only be revealed to us in another realm. Let us step into the future with confidence and hope in God.

Looking in Two Directions

Ephesians 1:3-14

Introduction
One of the important lessons I taught my children when they were young was how to cross a street. I always told them the importance of looking to the right and to the left before entering a street or highway. As they began driving I emphasized how important it is for them to keep their eyes on the road in front and to watch the mirrors for traffic behind or beside them. The apostle Paul is stressing the importance of looking in two directions spiritually. He tells us it is helpful to look backward to the past, but we must also look forward to the future. The writer of Ephesians takes a hopeful forward look at God's intentions for humanity and finds a remarkable vision. Paul encourages us.

I. We Are to Live According to His Plan (v. 11)
  A. God wants to bless us with every spiritual blessing.
  B. We see those blessings:
   1. Verse 4—Our blessings go back before the beginning of time.
   2. Verses 5-6—What a fantastic thing. We are members of the family of God, made to be partakers of the divine nature.
   3. Verses 7-8—Think of that! Redeemed and forgiven. Our guilt is removed, utterly gone.
   4. Verses 9-10—We have been taken into the secret counsels of the Almighty. He has unfolded to us what He plans to accomplish.

II. We Are to Live Through His Power (v. 11)
  A. Everything is going to be accomplished through the power of Christ and His Spirit living in us.
  B. Whatever God plans, He energizes.
  C. "Being confident of this, that he who began a good work in you will carry it on to completion until the day of Christ Jesus" (Phil. 1:6).
  D. What God starts, He finishes!

E. We are to live not only through His power but also through the presence of the Holy Spirit (vv. 13-14).

III. We Are to Live for His Praise (v. 12)
   A. We are to give Him the praise that He deserves.
      1. Everything occurs to the praise of God's glory.
      2. In order that God should be praised.
   B. We are to be filled with His Spirit so that we might be a reflection of His love and grace.

Conclusion

We need to keep our eyes open and our minds attentive to safely navigate an automobile on the streets and the highways. We also need to keep our spiritual eyes open and our minds attentive to what God is saying and where He is leading us in our lives.

The Power of the Resurrection

Ephesians 1:15-23

Introduction
Watches, cars, and Christians can all look chromed and shiny. But watches don't move, cars don't go, and Christians don't make a difference without something powering them. Paul tells us that as Christians we are powered and motivated by what we have in Christ Jesus.

I. **The Hope: The Hope to Which He Has Called Us (v. 18)**
   A. Before we came to know Christ, we were lost and without hope (2:12).
      1. When we received Christ as our personal Savior, we received a "living hope" (1 Pet. 1:3-5).
      2. We have been called out of darkness into His marvelous light.
      3. It is not something vague or a wistful longing but something assured to us, guaranteed.
      4. We have been given a guarantee, an earnest, and a deposit of things to come (vv. 13-14).
   B. We have a hope of eternity in heaven.
      1. And that hope should be a dynamic force in our lives, encouraging us to be obedient, to be faithful and to be pure (1 John 2:28—3:2-3).
      2. We have the hope of one day seeing Jesus face-to-face, and that fact should motivate us to live like Him today. We have a hope and:

II. **The Riches: The Riches of His Glorious Inheritance in the Saints (v. 18)**
   A. It is true that we have an inheritance and riches in Christ.
      1. 1 Cor. 1:5
      2. 2 Cor. 8:9
      3. Col. 3:23-24
      4. 1 Pet. 1:3-4
      5. We are rich in Christ Jesus.

B. However, the correct interpretation of this verse is not that we *have* an inheritance but that we *are* the inheritance!
  C. God does not deal with us on the basis of our past or even our present, but on our future! We are His riches and He is ours!

III. **The Power: The Incomparably Great Power for Us Who Believe (vv. 19-23)**
  A. Paul wants us to know that we have an unlimited supply of power available.
    1. God has shown us His love by making us His inheritance.
    2. God has encouraged us by promising a wonderful future.
    3. Now He gives us strength and confidence and power by telling us about the incomparably great power, the exceeding greatness of His power to us who believe.
    4. He uses the word *dynamis* (power as in dynamite) and *energia* (word for "energy").
    5. Paul is talking about divine dynamite, eternal energy, and it is available to every Christian, even to us!
  B. Paul goes on to say that this strength and might of His power is seen in the resurrection of Jesus Christ (vv. 20-23).
    1. The power by which the dead, decaying corpse of Jesus was raised from the dead and exalted to life is the *same power that is at work within us!*
      a. It is the same power by which we can renounce the dominion of sin and walk in the newness of life.
      b. It is the same power by which we can defeat any spiritual foe that comes against us.
    2. Paul wants us to know the greatness of God's power, so that we will not fail to use our riches and the power that is available to us.

Conclusion
Paul's prayer is that we might know the hope, the riches, and the power!

Paul's Prayer for Enlightenment

Ephesians 1:15-23

Introduction
The late newspaper publisher William Randolph Hearst invested a fortune collecting art treasures from around the world. One day, Mr. Hearst found a description of some valuable items and felt that he must own them. He sent his agent overseas to find them. After months of searching, the agent reported that he had finally found the art treasures. They were in Mr. Hearst's warehouse.

He had been searching frantically for treasures that he already owned. Had he read the catalog of his own treasures, he would have saved a great deal of time and a great amount of money.

The apostle Paul desired that the Ephesian Christians might understand the great treasure they had in Christ Jesus. So in verses 15-23 he prays for them that they might have:

I. A Spirit of Wisdom (v. 17)
    A. Real wisdom comes by divine revelation.
    B. The Holy Spirit is the source of that revelation.
        1. He guides and teaches us.
        2. John 16:13
        3. 1 Cor. 2:10-16
    C. Paul desired that they might understand the doctrines of Christ.

II. An Enlightened Heart (v. 18)
    A. The heart is the core and center of life.
    B. The heart is the arena where the battle between sin and salvation is fought.
    C. Only as God enlightens the heart do we have a right concept of Him, turning us from the blindness of a darkened heart to make the correct decision to accept and follow Jesus.
    D. An enlightened heart enables us to know our hope.

III. A Glorious Inheritance (v. 18)
   A. Our spiritual inheritance is a gift to receive (2:8-9).
   B. Our spiritual inheritance is incomparable. Jesus offers a plethora of benefits to those who follow Him—peace of heart and mind, inexpressible joy, indescribable love, unlimited mercy and grace, eternal life, just to name a few.
   C. Our spiritual inheritance is incomprehensible.
      1. 1 Cor. 2:9-10
      2. Our inheritance is both present and future.

IV. A Mighty Power (vv. 19-23)
   A. Paul prays that they might not only have wisdom, enlightenment, and an inheritance but also have the power to enjoy them.
   B. Paul is praying for spiritual dynamite and eternal energy.
   C. Paul gives an illustration of this power (vv. 20-22).

Conclusion
The power that raised Jesus from the dead is the same power that works in us. It is the same power by which we can repudiate the dominion of sin and walk in the newness of life. We can defeat any spiritual force or foe, because of God's power in us. Paul wants us to know the greatness of God's power so we will not fail to use our wealth and the power that is available. Paul's prayer for us is that we might know God's calling, experience God's riches, and possess God's power.

Our Authority in Christ

Ephesians 1:18—2:7

Introduction
Many great prayers have been prayed:
  The Lord's Prayer
  The Serenity Prayer
    God grant me the serenity
    To accept the things I cannot change,
    The courage to change the things I can,
    And the wisdom to know the difference.
  Francis of Assisi prayed:
  Lord, make me an instrument of your peace!
    Where there is hatred, let me sow love;
    Where there is injury, pardon;
    Where there is doubt, faith;
    Where there is despair, hope;
    Where there is darkness, light;
    And where there is sadness, joy.
  O Divine Master, grant that I may not so much seek
    To be consoled as to console;
    To be understood as to understand;
    To be loved as to love;
    For it is in giving that we receive;
    It is in pardoning that we are pardoned;
    It is in dying that we are born to eternal life.

In Eph. 1, Paul prays a great prayer for the church at Ephesus and for all Christians. He prays that we might realize:

I. Our Calling (1:18-19)
  A. What is our hope?
    1. Man was originally made for authority and created for dominion.
    2. Man was originally given rulership and control of the earth.
    3. Gen. 1:26-30; Ps. 8:4-8
  B. But notice what happened.

II. Our Condition (2:1-3)
A. Man transferred his allegiance from God to Satan.
   1. How did we get in this condition?
   2. It began in the garden with the fall of Adam and Eve (Gen. 3:1-7, 21-24).
   3. Humanity is now blind to this calling (2 Cor. 4:4).
B. Man transferred the title for dominion of this earth to Satan.
   1. The only way God could legally recover it was through a man.
   2. A man on whom Satan had no claim, no control, no power.
   3. A man in whom Satan could find no sin.
   4. Jesus came to be our Redeemer and Christ.

III. Our Christ (2:4-5)
A. Jesus Christ came to be our Savior.
   1. He was tempted and tried.
   2. He was persecuted and crucified.
B. Through His death came our triumph (vv. 20-22).
   1 The cross of Christ canceled all of Satan's claims upon man and the earth.
   2. Satan has absolutely no rights upon anyone or anything.
      a. Heb. 2:14
      b. 1 John 3:8
      c. Matt. 28:18

IV. The Church (1:22; 2:6, 10)
A. Our responsibility
   1. Satan was completely and legally destroyed, but like all legal claims and transactions, Calvary's legal victory must be enforced!
   2. The enforcement is in the hands of the church.
      a. Matt. 16:18-19
      b. Luke 10:17-19
B. Our reign
   1. One day we will reign with Christ.
   2. We are now in training, apprenticeship, being prepared for our royal role.

Conclusion

Our on-the-job training for eternal cosovereignty with Christ, for overcoming the evil forces in this world, for the enforcement of His will on earth, and for doing all that God wants us to do is prayer. Prayer releases God's Spirit into action to confront and conquer Satan. Prayer shapes and regulates the world. Prayer enforces God's will on earth. We have the key—it is prayer. We have the privilege, the responsibility, the authority to enforce God's will and administer His decisions.

Taking Off Your Graveclothes

Ephesians 2:1-10

Introduction
On many occasions Jesus found a place of rest and sweet fellowship in the home of Lazarus and his sisters, Mary and Martha. Whenever He was near the town of Bethany, He made His way to their house. Jesus loved Lazarus, Mary, and Martha. One day as Jesus was preaching in a nearby town, the urgent news came, Lazarus was seriously ill. However, Jesus delayed His return to Bethany. By the time He arrived, Lazarus was dead—buried in the graveyard for four days.

Upon arriving in Bethany, Jesus saw the heartbreak of Lazarus's friends and sisters. Moved with compassion, Jesus approached the grave of Lazarus and ordered the stone rolled away. He prayed to God and then spoke in a loud voice: "Lazarus, come out!" To the amazement of everyone, the dead man, Lazarus, came walking out. His hands and feet were still wrapped in the linen graveclothes and his face covered with the burial cloth. Jesus said to the stunned mourners: "Take off his graveclothes, let him go, he is alive!" Lazarus was once dead and was now alive! What a difference Jesus makes. Lazarus was taken out of the graveyard and placed into fellowship with Jesus. What a miracle!

There is a miracle that Jesus wants to do in every person's life. He desires to take spiritually dead sinners out of the graveyard of sin and place them into the throne room of God's glory. In this passage Paul shows us how we are made alive in Christ.

I. Our Situation
  A. We are dead in our sins (v. 1).
   1. Sinners are spiritually dead!
   2. The cause of death is sin (Rom. 6:23).
  B. We are disobedient (v. 2).
   1. They followed the ways of the world. The world puts pressure upon us to conform to its values, standards, attitudes, and actions (Rom. 12:1-2).
   2. They followed the ruler of the kingdom of the air.

   a. Satan uses things to influence the lives of sinners.
   b. Satan uses habits and hobbies to divert our attention from God.
  3. They followed their own sinful nature.
   a. Why does a sinner behave like a sinner? The sinful nature.
   b. A sinner is controlled by the world, the devil, and his or her own sinful nature.
 C. We are doomed (v. 3).
  1. A sinner's sentence is already passed—death.
  2. But God in His mercy is staying the execution of the sentence.
   a. Verse 1—the sinner is dead, but God!
   b. Verse 2—the sinner is disobedient, but God!
   c. Verse 3—the sinner is doomed, but God!
   d. God steps in to save the sinner.

II. Our Salvation
 A. He loves us (v. 4).
  1. God is rich in mercy.
  2. God does not give us what we deserve—eternal punishment.
  3. God gives us what we do not deserve—eternal life (Rom. 5:8-9).
 B. He made us alive (v. 5).
  1. Jesus brought physical resurrection to Lazarus.
  2. Jesus brings spiritual resurrections to sinners.
  3. Jesus gives us a new life, a new nature, a new beginning, and a new relationship with God.
 C. He raised us (v. 6).
  1. We are not raised and left in the graveyard.
  2. We are made alive and united with Christ.
  3. We are exalted with Christ.
  4. We share His throne, His riches, and His power.

III. Our Service
 A. God's work in us (v. 10*a*).
 B. God's work through us (v. 10*b*).

Conclusion
Are you enjoying the liberty you have in Christ? Are you living as one who has been made alive, raised up, and exalted with Christ? Are you allowing God to work in and through you? If not, take off the graveclothes of the past and enjoy the new life Christ has for you.

God's Workmanship

Ephesians 2:10

Introduction
Dennis Waitley has written a national best-seller titled *Seeds of Greatness: The Ten Best-Kept Secrets of Total Success!* He discovered from top executives, Olympics athletes, prisoners of war, and scientists 10 simple but profound secrets for living a fruitful, happy, and successful life. He says, "These ten basic truths help you discover, nurture, and actualize your real resources to do exactly what you want to do in your life. I think we are all interested in living a fruitful, happy, and successful life at work, home, and church."

How can we be the best we can be? I would like to share with you from God's best-selling book, the Bible, the three best-kept secrets of total success in our Christian life.

I. Statement of God's Power ("We are God's workmanship")
  A. We, who were created by God in His image, were spoiled by sin.
  B. Our lives were marred and ruined by sin and failure.
   1. We were dead (2:1).
   2. We were disobedient (2:2).
   3. We were depraved (2:3).
   4. We were doomed (2:12).
   5. We were destroyed.
  C. But we are destined to become the very special expression of God's creative power.
   1. We who were destroyed and marred and ruined by sin have been made anew by God into His masterpiece.
   2. We who were dead, He has made alive (2:4).
   3. We who were disobedient, He has chosen to be holy and blameless (1:4).
   4. We who were depraved, He has lavished with wisdom and understanding (1:8).

5. We who were demonized, He has given His Spirit (1:13).
        6. We who were doomed, He has given new life (2 Cor. 5:17).
        7. We are God's masterpieces, His workmanship.
   II. **Statement of God's Purpose** ("created for good works")
        A. We are created to do works.
            1. We were not only created to "be" but also to "do."
            2. We have the wonderful privilege of doing things for God.
        B. We are called to do good works.
   III. **Statement of God's Preparation** ("prepared in advance for us to do")
        A. God has a plan for each one of our lives, and He wants us to walk in His will and fulfill His plan.
        B. God has prepared in advance work that He desires for us to do.
            1. Think about that truth.
            2. There is a job that God has just for me!
            3. Our responsibility is to be open, available, and ready when He calls.

Conclusion

God has worked for us through His creative power. God has worked in us for a divine purpose. God wants to work through us to accomplish the things He has prepared for us to accomplish. May Frances R. Havergal's prayer be our prayer:

> Take my life and let it be
> Consecrated, Lord, to Thee.
> . . . .
> Take my hands, and let them move
> At the impulse of Thy love.

Grace—Past, Present, Future

Ephesians 2:11-22

Introduction
Have you been to one of your class reunions from high school or college? Those reunions are times of laughter, joy, surprise, shock, and even sadness. In preparation for a class reunion, a person might get out the old yearbooks and look back through the pictures. It's a time one tries to recall names and faces.

Looking back through the yearbooks brought a smile to my face and laughter to my heart as I remembered people and activities. The experience brought joyful memories. In Eph. 2:11-22, the apostle Paul gives us things to ponder.

I. Remembering Our Past (vv. 11-12)
  A. Separation
    1. We were separated from God.
    2. We were excluded from citizenship.
    3. We were foreigners to the covenant of promise.
  B. Situation
    1. We were without hope.
    2. We were without God.
    3. We need to remember where we were before we met Christ.

II. Pondering Our Present (vv. 13-18)
  A. Brought near through His blood (v. 13).
    1. Pardon and forgiveness (Rom. 5:9; 1 Pet. 1:18-19; Rev. 1:5)
    2. Purity (Heb. 9:14; 1 John 1:7)
  B. Barriers are removed by His body (vv. 14-18). We have access to the Father (Eph. 3:12; Heb. 10:19-22).

III. Anticipating Our Future (vv. 19-22)
  A. Relationship to God (vv. 19-21)
    1. Believers are no longer aliens, but fellow citizens and members of God's family (John 1:12; Rom. 8:15-17; 1 John 3:1).

      2. We are united with the apostles, prophets, and Jesus Christ.
  B. Believers become the residence of the Holy Spirit (v. 22). We are the dwelling place of the Holy Spirit (Gal. 2:20; Eph. 3:17; Col. 1:27; 1 Cor. 3:16; 6:19).

Conclusion

The provisions of God's great salvation are marvelous to ponder. I challenge you to spend time in His Word and in His presence considering the past life He brought you from, pondering what grace is doing for your life in the present, and anticipating the future He has for you in Him.

A Mystery Revealed

Ephesians 3:1-13

Introduction
The apostle Paul wrote this letter while he was a prisoner in Rome awaiting trial before Nero. He was waiting for the Jewish prosecutors to come with their hatred and malicious charges. In prison, Paul had certain privileges. He was allowed to stay in a house that he had rented. He was allowed visits from his friends. However, he was still a prisoner. He was chained to the wrist of a Roman soldier whose responsibility was to prevent his escape.

Paul never thought of himself as a prisoner of Rome. He always thought of himself as a prisoner of Christ. He never considered himself to be a victim of men but a champion for Christ. In this section Paul returns to the thought that is at the very heart of this letter. Into his life had come the revelation of the great secret and mystery of God. The mystery was: the love and mercy and grace of God were meant not only for the Jews but for all humankind (Acts 26:18).

Paul was sent by God to open the eyes of the Gentiles, so they would turn from darkness to the light and from the power of Satan to God. This was a new discovery.

I. The Mystery Was Revealed to Paul (vv.1-5)
   A. Paul was called.
      1. The mystery was made known to Paul through a revelation.
      2. Paul was to make the mystery known to the Gentiles.
   B. Paul was courageous.
      1. He defended it before the church.
      2. He debated it with the world.
      3. He delivered the mystery wherever he went.

II. The Mystery Revealed by Paul to the Gentiles (vv. 6-8)
   A. Gentiles became heirs (v. 6).
   B. Gentiles became members of one body (v. 6).
      1. Gentiles are given a new relationship (v. 6).

       2. Gentiles are given the riches of Christ (v. 8).
       3. Gentiles are given a new power (v. 7).
III. **The Mystery Revealed Through the Church (vv. 10-13)**
    A. Our responsibility
       1. When God saved Paul, He deposited with him the precious treasures of the gospel truth.
       2. Paul committed these truths to the faithful men who guarded and shared them (1 Tim. 6:20; 2 Tim. 2:2; 4:7).
       3. We are the stewards of this great mystery.
       4. It is our responsibility to share the Good News with all people (v. 9).
    B. Our resources
       1. Authority—confidence and courage (v. 12).
       2. Access—we have access to the Father.

Conclusion

One of the reasons many Christians are weak and ineffective is they do not understand what they have in Christ. They do not realize what He has done for them. The Good News is still a mystery and a secret to them. As we grasp the inside story, the mystery, we must share the Good News with others. We must spread the word to our world, so that everyone can hear the message.

Paul's Prayer for Enablement

Ephesians 3:1, 14-21

Introduction
Some people go to prison as amateurs in crime and come out skilled professionals in crime. Others use their time more profitably. John Bunyan was imprisoned over a period of 12 years in the 17th century. While he was a prisoner, he wrote his masterpiece, *Pilgrim's Progress*. Ferdinand Marcos was imprisoned in his native Philippines. He studied law with such success that he defended himself against murder charges and was acquitted. He later became president of the Philippines. Chuck Colson was imprisoned for his involvement in the Watergate cover-up. While in prison, Colson became a Christian and wrote his best-selling book *Born Again*.

The apostle Paul, a prisoner in Rome, used his time wisely. He wrote his prison Epistles, the doctrine of the Church. He was involved in evangelistic activities and discipleship training. One area of his prison life that should not be overlooked was his prayer life. These verses of chapter 3 contain Paul's second prayer for the church at Ephesus. In his first prayer, he prayed for their enlightenment. In this second prayer, he is praying for their enablement.

I. He Prays for Their Spiritual Strength (v. 16)
   A. Our spiritual power and strength come from a continuous reliance on the Holy Spirit.
   B. We receive the power of the Holy Spirit when we ask for it (Luke 11:11-13).
      1. J. Hudson Taylor, missionary to China, wrote: "All God's giants have been weak men who did great things for God because they relied upon His power and His presence through prayer."
      2. The Holy Spirit will enable us to know God's love (v. 18).

II. He Prays That We May Know God's Love (vv. 17*b*-19)
   A. Paul's concern is that we might not just appreciate God's love but that we may grasp, lay hold of the vast expanses of the love of Christ.

B. To fulfill His purpose and plan we need to be rooted and grounded in His love (v. 17).
      1. Rooted—an agricultural term
      2. Grounded—an architectural term
      3. Christ's continuous presence that comes through prayer and a rooting and grounding in His love will help us experience God's fullness.

III. **He Prays That We Might Experience God's Fullness (v. 19b)**
   A. The means of our fullness—the Holy Spirit (Eph. 5:18)
      1. 2 Pet. 1:3-4
      2. John Fletcher noted: "We must not be content to be cleansed from sin; we must be filled with His fullness."
   B. The measure of our fullness—God himself
      1. He is the unlimited source from which we draw all the spiritual resources that we need.
      2. We are filled with the fullness of God as we yield ourselves to Him.
      3. Dwight L. Moody once gave an illustration of God's fullness. He held up a glass and said, "Tell me, how can I get the air out of the glass I have in my hand?" One man said, "Suck it out with a pump." The evangelist replied, "That would create a vacuum and shatter the glass." After many suggestions, Moody picked up a pitcher and quietly filled the glass with water. "There," he said, "all the air is now removed."
      4. As we are filled with the Holy Spirit, sinful self will be cleansed.

Conclusion

Paul concludes this prayer with a great doxology. "Now unto him that is able to do exceedingly abundantly above all we ask or think" (3:20, KJV). Paul uses every word possible to convey the vastness of God's power as found in Christ Jesus. We cannot ask beyond God's ability to fulfill. God is exceeding abundantly able to fill us with himself. The power is available. It is not a luxury but a necessity. Let us pray: "Lord, give me spiritual strength in my inner being by Your Holy Spirit; give me spiritual apprehension so that I might know Your great love. Lord, fill me with Your fullness today!"

Living a Worthy Life

Ephesians 4:1-16

Introduction
All of Paul's letters contain a beautiful balance between doctrine and duty. The Book of Ephesians is a perfect example. The first three chapters deal with doctrine: our spiritual riches. The last three chapters explain our duty: our spiritual responsibility in Christ.

In this passage Paul admonishes us to live a life worthy of our calling as Christians. The main idea in the first 16 verses is the unity of believers. This is really the practical application of the doctrine taught in chapter 1. We are called to be people who build bridges instead of barriers. We are called to operate on the basis of service rather than selfishness. To live a life that is worthy requires that we live in unity with one another.

I. The Ground of Our Unity (vv. 4-6)
   A. Some people say that it is not important what you believe as long as you love one another and live a good life. It does make a difference, because what you believe will determine how you behave.
   B. Paul lays the foundation and names seven basic spiritual realities that unite all true believers.
      1. One Body—the Church (v. 4). Christ is the Head and the Church is the Body (see 1 Cor. 12:12-13).
      2. One Spirit—the Holy Spirit activates the fellowship. When we are filled with the same Spirit, there should be no hardness or division, but peace and unity.
      3. One hope of your calling—we have a glorious future (v. 4). We are all proceeding toward the same goal. We should all be committed to the same cause.
      4. One Lord—Christ to whom we all belong.
      5. One faith—singular commitment to Christ; complete surrender to the love of Christ Jesus.
      6. One baptism—sign of entry into the Church.
      7. One God and Father—He is our Father. In Ephesians, Paul refers to God as Father five times (1:3, 17; 2:18;

3:14; 5:20). Jesus taught us to pray, "Our Father," not "My Father." There should be a oneness in the family of God.

II. The Grace of Our Unity (vv. 1-3)
A. To live a worthy life and live in unity requires some unusual qualities; we must possess Christian graces.
B. We should be:
 1. Humble—putting Christ first, others second, and self last.
 2. Gentle—every instinct and passion under control.
 3. Patient—one who bears insult and injury without bitterness and complaint.
 4. Loving—bearing one another in love.
 5. Peaceful—the right relationship between persons.

III. The Gifts of Unity (vv. 7-11)
A. Paul moves in these verses from what all Christians have in common to how Christians differ from each other.
 1. God has given each believer spiritual gifts.
 2. These gifts are to be used for the unifying and edifying of the Body of Christ.
 3. There are three different lists of spiritual gifts in the New Testament: 1 Cor. 12:4-11; Rom. 12:3-8; and Eph. 4:11.
 4. Paul lists here not so much the gifts as the gifted persons God has placed in the church.
    a. Apostle—one sent with a commission; a divinely appointed representative.
    b. Prophet—proclaimer of the Word of God.
    c. Evangelist—bearer of the good news; these persons traveled from place to place preaching the gospel and leading people to Christ.
    d. Pastor and teacher—one office with two ministries.
       (1) Pastor means shepherd. His or her responsibility is to feed and lead the flock.
       (2) A teacher had the responsibility for telling the story of Jesus.
B. Every believer has a ministry that will strengthen the church.

IV. The Goal of Unity (vv. 12-16)
   A. Produce maturity.
   B. Prepare ministers.
   C. Provide spiritual growth.

Conclusion

Every Christian has a ministry no matter how insignificant he or she may think it is. The Body grows as individual members grow. If one Christian fails to develop spiritually, the whole Church is not as strong as it ought to be. By growing spiritually, the unity of the Body is preserved, the witness of the Church is maintained, and the growth of the Church is accomplished.

Off with the Old; on with the New!

Ephesians 4:17-32

Introduction
In this portion of Scripture Paul returns to the thought of 2:1-10. In chapter 2 we saw that by God's grace the spiritually dead sinner is taken out of the graveyard of sin and death and placed in the throne room of God's glory. Therefore, in light of what he wrote in chapter 2, we are told to take off the old man and put on the new man. We are to take off the clothes of the old life and put on the clothes of our new life in Christ.

I. The Old Life Characterized (vv. 17-19)
   A. Thinking is futile (v. 17).
      1. The thinking of the unsaved is radically different from Christians.
      2. Their thinking is futile, purposeless, aimless, and useless.
      3. They cannot truly understand themselves, the world, or the things of God.
      4. They have no spiritual wisdom.
   B. Thinking is darkened (v. 18).
      1. Rom. 1:22-23
      2. 2 Cor. 4:3-4
      3. They cannot see the truth of Jesus Christ.
      4. They cannot think straight or rationally about eternal things.
   C. Thinking is ignorant (v. 18).
      1. This is a frightening sentence.
      2. They have lost all sensitivity and have become hardened.
      3. They have given themselves over to outrageous sensuality, uncleanness, and greed.
   D. Thinking of the Christian described.
      1. Thinking is not futile, but purposeful.
      2. Thinking is filled not with darkness, but with light.
      3. Thinking is not ignorant, but we are filled with spiritual wisdom.

II. The New Life Commanded (vv. 20-24)
   A. Put off the old self.
      1. Salvation goes much deeper than just changing our minds; it changes our whole life.
      2. Take off the old self; put on the new self.
      3. Gal. 2:20
      4. 2 Cor. 5:17
   B. Renew the mind (v. 23).
      1. Present infinitive—a process.
      2. A continuous renewing of our spiritual lives by the Holy Spirit as we surrender to Him.
      3. The Word of God renews our minds as we surrender to Him day by day.
      4. As we meditate on the Word of God, the Holy Spirit gradually transforms our lives into the image of Jesus Christ.
      5. Phil. 4:8-9
   C. Put on the new man (v. 24).
      1. Col. 3:10
      2. Rom. 13:14
      3. Gal. 3:27
      4. Through the enabling of the Holy Spirit we can continue in our lives of obedience and faith until we stand complete in our surrender and complete to the will of God.
      5. 1 Thess. 5:23-24

Conclusion

It is time to take off the clothes of the old life and put on the clothes of the new life. It is time to stop carrying around the unnecessary weights of besetting sins. It is time to begin to live the life that God has for every one of His children. It is time for our minds and thinking to be changed. It is time for our hearts to be filled and empowered by the Holy Spirit. It is time for us to be holy as He is holy. Peter wrote in 1 Pet. 1:14-16: "As obedient children, do not conform to the evil desires you had when you lived in ignorance. But just as he who called you is holy, so be holy in all you do; for it is written: 'Be holy, because I am holy.'"

Directives for the New Life

Ephesians 4:25—5:2

Introduction
In chapter 4 we are urged to live a life worthy of our high calling. In verses 17-24, Paul exhorts the readers to put away the old life, the old self, and to put on the new life, the new self. Now in 4:25—5:2, Paul gives a list of directives. He lists some vices to avoid and some virtues to apply to our new life in Christ.

It is not surprising that Christians in the first century just emerging from paganism and surrounded by degrading customs needed such warnings and admonitions. But we must admit that believers in the present day with all our advantages need them as well. In these eight verses Paul gives in rapid-fire succession six injunctions that relate to the new nature that they have put on and to the new life in Christ. These are implications and consequences of having put off the old man.

Paul is saying, "Now that you are new men, live your lives this way."

I. **Our Speech (4:25, 29)**
   A. We are to put away lying.
      1. A lie is a statement contrary to fact that is spoken with the intent to deceive.
      2. Whenever we lie, Satan goes to work.
      3. The first sin judged in the Early Church was lying (Acts 5:1-11).
   B. Our lives as Christians should be controlled by truth.
      1. We belong to each other.
      2. We are members of one Body.
      3. We are to build the Body in love (Eph. 4:16) and in truth (v. 15).
      4. Speak the truth in love.

II. **Our Anger (vv. 26-27)**
   A. Anger in itself is not a sin.
      1. It is possible to be angry and not sin, but very difficult.

  2. Paul sets a definite limitation of time to deal with your anger (v. 26).
  3. If the fire of anger is not quenched by loving forgiveness, it will spread and defile and destroy God's work.
  4. Anger gives the devil a foothold in our lives.
  5. When he finds a believer with a spark of anger in his heart, he fans those sparks, adds fuel to the fire, and tries to do a great deal of damage to God's people, church, and testimony.
 B. Allow the Holy Spirit to remove your anger.
  1. Do not suppress anger.
  2. Do not let it smolder indefinitely.

III. Our Work (v. 28)
 A. We are directed to work.
 B. We are to work to glorify God and to give to others.

IV. Our Attitude (vv. 30-32)
 A. Our mouth and our heart are connected (Matt. 12:34).
  1. An ancient proverb says: "The heart of man is a well. The mouth of a man is a bucket. That which is in the well of the heart can be determined by what is in the bucket of the mouth."
  2. When we become Christians, our speech and attitudes should change.
 B. The remedy for corrupt speech and a critical spirit is to fill the heart with praise and blessing.
  1. Fill your heart with the love of Christ, so that only truth and purity come out of your mouth.
  2. Build up one another.

V. Our Compassion and Forgiveness (v. 32)
 A. Resentment will create bitterness and will poison the whole inner man.
 B. Resentment grieves the Holy Spirit.
 C. We are to forgive as Christ has forgiven us and love others as Christ has loved us.

Conclusion
 We are to live as Christ lived. After all, we have been raised from spiritual death. Let us live like it.

Imitating Our Father

Ephesians 5:1-17

Introduction
In this passage Paul sets before us the highest standard in the entire world. He tells us to be imitators of God. This passage is based on three admonitions.

I. Live a Life of Love (vv. 1-2)
    A. Be rooted and grounded in love.
        1. In the Epistle, Paul has already:
            a. Prayed that we might be rooted and grounded in love (3:17).
            b. Told us to speak the truth in love (4:15).
            c. Told us to be built up in love (4:16).
        2. Now he urges us as beloved children to make our whole lives a reflection, a demonstration of the love of God.
    B. Reflect His love.
        1. The starting place is the example of Christ.
        2. We are to follow Christ's example and love people with the same sacrificial love with which Jesus loved and forgave them.
    C. Resemble Christ.

II. Live as Children of Light (vv. 3-14)
Since God is light and we are imitators of our Father, then we should walk in light and have nothing to do with the darkness of sin. Paul gives three descriptions of believers.
    A. Live as holy people (vv. 3-4).
        1. We are set apart to be saints.
        2. We have been called out of the darkness into His marvelous light (1 Pet. 2:9).
        3. It is beneath the dignity of a holy saint to indulge in the sins that belong to the world of darkness.
    B. Live as heirs of His kingdom (vv. 5-6).
    C. Live as halogen lamps (light) (vv. 8-14).
        1. By grace, we have become partakers of the light, so we should have nothing to do with the darkness of sin.

2. We are to shine brightly like a halogen lamp.
3. As Christians, as lights we should have three effects:
   a. Light produces fruit (v. 9).
      (1) Light is essential for photosynthesis to occur, through which plants draw nutrients from the air and soil.
      (2) As we walk in the light, we will produce spiritual fruit.
      (3) As we live as light, we produce the fruit of righteousness and goodness in our world.
   b. Light tests acceptability (v. 10).
      (1) We should live openly before God (Heb. 4:13).
      (2) Airport security scanners show everything in a suitcase.
      (3) It is great to be able to live our spiritual lives not being ashamed or hiding anything from God.
      (4) All of our lives should be lived in the light of God's approval and acceptance.
   c. Light reproves (vv. 11-13).
      (1) Satan and sin blind the mind of the unsaved.
      (2) By our character and conduct we bring God's light into a dark world.
      (3) By our testimony and witness we can share Christ with others.
      (4) We are called to be lights in our world—let your light shine!

Conclusion

We are holy people—partakers of the inheritance of the saints. We are heirs—delivered from the power of darkness and translated into the kingdom of God. We are lights—bringing light into our dark world. Let's imitate our Father.

Imitators of God

Ephesians 5:1-2

Introduction
Rich Little and other comedians have made a career of imitating others. We laugh at their jokes and the copying of mannerisms of presidents, candidates, athletes, and other celebrities.

I. Whether We Will Admit It or Even Recognize It— We Are All Imitators
   A. We imitate our parents.
      1. Things we promised we would never do or say to our own children, we do and say just like our parents.
      2. We look like them, act like them, even talk like them.
   B. We imitate our friends.
      1. The clothes they wear.
      2. The cars they drive.
      3. The values they live.
   C. We imitate our heroes or people we admire.
      We are all imitators, so we need to be careful what we imitate.

II. We Need to Be Careful Whom We Choose to Imitate
   A. Our lives will become a reflection of whom we imitate.
      1. That is why Paul in Eph. 5:1 wrote, "Be imitators of God!"
      2. There are few more discouraging experiences than trying to emulate the example of an expert when you barely qualify as an amateur.
   B. How can we possibly imitate God?

III. Paul Wrote, "Be Imitators of God"—That Sounds Impossible!
   A. It is hard enough to grasp His greatness; to comprehend His character, and His attributes are beyond scope even to measure, much less be imitated.
   B. I guess I could try to imitate Him on the surface, on the outside.

    C. But the problem is not so much on the outside, but being an imitator of God on the inside.
        1. My biggest challenge comes when I read Eph. 4:21-32.
        2. How does Paul expect us to really be imitators of a perfect, Holy God?

IV. Our Imitation of God Starts with a Realization That God Loves Us (vv. 30, 32)
    A. When He offered himself up, the Just for the unjust, love attained its climax, its maximum.
    B. The amazingly large debt we could never pay—was forgiven.

V. Because We Are Loved by the Father and Are Forgiven Our Sins, We Are to Imitate Him by Living a Life of Love and Forgiveness (5:1)
    A. Our forgiveness of wrongs is to be as ungrudging as our Heavenly Father's forgiveness of our wrongs.
    B. Our dealings and interactions with others are to be molded on the basis of God's dealings with us.
    C. We are to treat our fellow debtors as we have been treated (Matt. 18:21-35).

Conclusion

Before coming to power, Louis XII of France had been cast into prison and kept in chains. Later when he became king, he was urged to seek revenge on the people who put him into prison, but he refused. Instead, he prepared a scroll on which he listed all the people who had committed crimes against him. Behind every man's name he placed a cross in red ink. When the guilty heard about this, they feared for their lives and fled. Then the king explained, "The cross which I drew beside each name was not a sign of punishment, but a pledge of forgiveness extended for the sake of the crucified Savior, who upon His cross forgave His enemies and prayed for them and who forgave me." We imitate our Heavenly Father as we live a life of love and forgiveness just as we have been loved and forgiven by God our Father.

Always Giving Thanks

Ephesians 5:15-20

Introduction
A mother said to her minister upon the recovery of her child from a serious illness, "Wasn't God good to give us back our child?" He was about to agree with her when a thought came to him as never before. To her surprise he said, "Yes, but would not God have been just as good, or just as kind, if your child had not come back to you." Her answer was doubtful and without enthusiasm.

It is easy to give God thanks and to speak of God's goodness when we are having our wishes granted and everything is going our way. But we must realize that we are to thank God for all things.

The apostle Paul tells us in Eph. 5 to give thanks always to God. In 1 Thess. 5:18 we are instructed by Paul to give thanks in all circumstances, for this is God's will for you in Christ Jesus. How can we give thanks always and in all circumstances?

I. **Because We Know God Cares**
   A. God knows about every part of our lives, and He cares about every part of our lives.
   B. If God cares, then why do bad things happen?
   C. We live in a fallen and sinful world.
   D. However, we can still be thankful, because He suffers with us and He promises us victory.
   E. Rom. 8:28 is our promise, so be thankful in the midst of all circumstances.

II. **Because There Is Renewal in Thanksgiving (v. 19)**
   A. Thanksgiving brings us to a place of rest and renewal.
      1. "Those who hope in the Lord will renew their strength" (Isa. 40:31).
      2. "Be still, and know that I is God" (Ps. 46:10).
   B. When we reflect on God's blessings and praise Him, burdens will be lifted.

III. Because Thanksgiving Keeps Life in Perspective
   A. Thieves once robbed Matthew Henry, the famous scholar. He wrote in his diary:
   > Let me be thankful first:
   > Because I was never robbed before.
   > Because although they took my wallet, they did not take my life.
   > Because although they took my wallet; it was not much.
   > Because it was I who was robbed, not I who robbed.

   B. His spirit of thanksgiving gave him a new perspective on his difficulties.
   C. When we give thanks in the midst of life, we will gain a new perspective.
   D. The Psalmist David in the midst of conflict wrote Ps. 103. Taking the time to read verses 1-5 and verses 10-13 will help us give thanks.

Conclusion

Thanksgiving gives us a confidence in the present situations of life and a hope for our futures. Take some time to give Him thanks.

In Holy Communion we stop and reflect upon what God has done for us in Christ Jesus. As we reflect, we realize that it is through the shedding of His blood that we have received every spiritual blessing. Let's be thankful for what God has done for us through Jesus Christ. Let's take the time to reflect, thank, and praise God.

LIFE CAN BE GLORIOUSLY FULL

Ephesians 5:15-20

Introduction
In southern New Jersey, the Betsy Ross Bridge crosses the Delaware River. The bridge is a spectacular sight with eight lanes arching gracefully over the river. The cost was $105 million at the time of its construction. It is called the "Bridge to Nowhere." It was to connect to an interstate, but the interstate was never built, so the bridge literally goes nowhere.

Many in our world are going nowhere. Many are spending their lives building bridges to nowhere. The apostle Paul says in Eph. 5 that the bridge that really takes a person somewhere is the infilling of the Holy Spirit. He tells us how we can live a life that is gloriously full.

I. Filled with the Spirit (v. 18)
   A. The Holy Spirit is God's stamp of ownership on us (Eph. 1:13-14).
   B. The Holy Spirit is the Guarantee that we shall receive His promises (1:13).
   C. The Holy Spirit is His power working in us (1:17-19). What a staggering truth that the very same power that raised Jesus from the dead is available to work in us.
   D. How are we filled with the Spirit?
      1. By praying and asking for Him (Luke 11:13).
      2. By continually allowing the Spirit to fill us (Eph. 3:19).

II. Filled with Song (v. 19)
   A. We Christians, who have been loved by God, accepted into His family, forgiven by His blood, empowered by His Spirit, should be filled with a song deep in our hearts.
   B. Paul and Silas in Acts 16:22-25.
   C. Jesus and the disciples in Matt. 26:30.
   D. During the western migration in America, a traveler on foot came to the bank of the frozen Mississippi River on a harsh, frigid winter afternoon. He was afraid to cross

on the ice, not knowing how thick it was. Nighttime was closing in as he hesitated. He dropped to his hands and knees and began to slowly crawl across the frozen river. As he reached the middle, he heard singing coming from the darkening night. He turned his head to see four horses pulling a wagon loaded with coal across the ice. The driver was singing his heart out.
   E. Some people crawl through life on hands and knees in fear and trembling while others sing even in the dark.
      1. The difference lies in what a person believes about God.
      2. Eph. 1:3-4

III. **Filled with Thanks (v. 20)**
   A. In Brooklyn a motorist was driving along and was amazed by the bumper sticker on the truck in front of him. It read, "A blind man is driving this truck." Out of curiosity he pulled up alongside the truck. The driver of the truck smiled, winked, and waved his hand toward the side door. There was a sign, "Superior Venetian Blind Company."
   B. Some people go through life blinded to the astounding riches of God's grace, His love working in their lives, and His providence bringing everything to their good (Rom. 8:28).
   C. Our lives should be filled with thanks (Col. 1:12-14).

Conclusion

Our lives can be gloriously full with the joy, peace, and fulfillment of the Holy Spirit. He fills the heart with songs of thanksgiving.

The Control of the Spirit

Ephesians 5:18

Introduction
Many Christians experience ups and downs in their walk with God. It does not have to be that way in our Christian lives. We can live with victory and experience a life of spiritual growth. Our great need is to allow the Holy Spirit total control in our lives. This is an important verse for us to consider in our study on the Holy Spirit.

I. The Process
   A. Crisis
      1. The crisis experience could be called the baptism with the Holy Spirit.
      2. The baptism with the Holy Spirit is a specific time in your life in which God through the Holy Spirit cleanses and purifies your sinful and carnal nature and the Spirit witnesses to you that He has done it.
      3. The baptism with the Holy Spirit gives us the power and boldness to witness and be what God intends for us to be.
      4. In chapter 5, the Ephesians believers had already received the baptism of the Spirit (1:13; 4:30).
   B. The Process
      1. The tense of the verb in verse 18 is most important.
      2. The word "filled" is in the continuous present tense.
      3. Be perpetually, continually, always filled with the Spirit.
      4. Let it continue, let it be your constant condition.
      5. Paul is commanding them to keep on being filled with the Spirit.

II. The Person
   A. The Holy Spirit is a Person who has a great influence in our lives.
   B. We are to be full of the Holy Spirit.
      1. What does it mean to be full of something?
      2. Thayer's Greek Lexicon reads, "What wholly takes possession of the mind is said to fill it."

  3. To be filled with something or someone is to say it has a controlling influence on you.
 C. Paul's analogy: "Be not drunk with wine which leads to debauchery, but be filled with the Spirit."
  1. A person who is drunk is under the influence of alcohol.
  2. The alcohol controls this person's mind, emotions, and will.
 D. Our minds, emotions, and will are to be under the influence of the Holy Spirit.

IV. The Presence
 A. How can one be continually filled with the Holy Spirit?
  1. It is not in our power to be saved or forgiven.
  2. It is not in our power to be baptized with the Holy Spirit and be cleansed and purified.
  3. It is our choice to go on being filled with the Holy Spirit.
 B. The conditions
  1. Negatively
   a. Do not grieve the Holy Spirit (4:30).
   b. Do not allow sin to remain in our lives.
  2. Positively
   a. Realize that He is within you.
   b. Desire for Him.
   c. Pay careful attention to His promptings.
    (1) Read the Word and pray.
    (2) Obey the Spirit.
    (3) Allow Him to lead and guide you.

Conclusion
  There are no shortcuts to living a victorious, Spirit-filled life. It requires a decision to totally surrender our minds, emotions, and wills to the control of the Holy Spirit. It requires a yielding to the continuous infilling by the Holy Spirit. It requires a daily dependence upon Him.

Life in the Spirit

Ephesians 5:18

Introduction
Nothing is more remarkable about the apostle Paul than the varied character of his ministry. He was at one and the same time an evangelist, a preacher, a founder of churches, a theologian, a teacher, and a tenderhearted and sympathetic pastor. His doctrinal teaching is incomparable. But equally remarkable is the way in which he shows and works out the implications of those doctrines. To Paul, Christianity is a life to be lived, not merely a philosophy to be taught.

He approaches a practical problem in Christian living through doctrine. He places every problem in the context of the whole body of Christian truth. So he says that the answer to problems in marriage, in the family, and at work is to live a Christian life in the Spirit. What picture does Paul give us of the Christian life?

I. It Is a Controlled Life
   A. It is a controlled and ordered life.
   B. It is the very reverse of the condition of a drunkard who has lost control and is controlled by alcohol.
   C. A Spirit-filled person has control of his or her tongue.
      1. Ps. 39:1
      2. James 1:26
      3. James 3:5-8
      4. One writer put it this way: "Unless we yield our tongues as instruments of righteousness to God, Satan will use them to his advantage and to our spiritual impoverishment."
   D. A Spirit-filled person has self-control.
      1. He can control his or her temper and anger.
      2. He can control his or her emotions and patience.
      3. He can control his or her mind and thoughts.
      4. He can control his or her money and spending.

II. It Is a Productive Life
   A. It is not a wasteful life, but a productive life.
      1. In Luke 15, the prodigal son lived a wasted life.
      2. He squandered his money, time, energies, purity, and morality and lost everything.
   B. The Spirit-filled life conserves, builds up, adds to, and preserves our life. It does not exhaust a man but energizes and gives him power to live a full and abundant life.

III. It Is a Positive Life
   A. Some believe that the Christian life is all about negatives.
      1. Must do this, can't do that.
      2. It is a life of living under rules and laws.
      3. It dulls the soul and robs it of all its vitality.
   B. The Spirit-filled life gives new life.
      1. We will never experience abundant life until we surrender everything to God.
      2. Then we can experience the happiness and contentment that comes from walking with God.

IV. It Is a Stimulating Life
   A. The Holy Spirit stimulates the mind and intellect.
      1. He wants us to grow in knowledge and in wisdom.
      2. We will grow as we study His Word and receive His wisdom.
   B. The Holy Spirit stimulates the heart and passions.
   C. The Holy Spirit opens our hearts to love others.
   D. The Holy Spirit enlarges our capacity to love others.

Conclusion

This Spirit-filled life is attainable for any Christian who is willing to surrender to the Lord Jesus, who will allow God to become more than just a resident, but become the ruler. As the Spirit controls us, we will experience the fullness of God in our lives. It is only then that we will experience a controlled, productive, positive, and stimulating life.

Guidelines for Spirit-Filled Homes—Part 1

Ephesians 5:18-33

Introduction
For millions of Americans, the home has turned into a battleground filled with violent assaults, beatings, and deaths. Herbert Lingren said, "You will be in less danger of experiencing physical abuse while walking the streets at one a.m. than being among friends and family at home." Many of our homes have become outposts of hell instead of parcels of paradise. No matter what the statistics or experts tell us about homes in our society, we can have heaven in our homes. As C. H. Spurgeon said, "We can have homes where angels might be asked to stay, and they would not find themselves out of place."

There is an ingredient that is necessary if we are to have these kinds of homes. It is the Holy Spirit. For it is only through the power of the Holy Spirit that we can walk in harmony in the relationships of the home. Paul tells us in verse 18 to be filled with the Spirit—to be constantly controlled by the Spirit in our minds, emotions, and will. Paul states three evidences of a Spirit-filled life.

I. **Spirit-Filled Christians Are Joyful (v. 19)**
   A. Christian joy is not a shallow emotion, not like a thermometer that rises and falls with the changing atmosphere of the home.
      1. Christian joy is a thermostat.
      2. It does not rise and fall with the circumstances.
      3. It determines the spiritual atmosphere.
   B. No matter what the circumstances are around them, Spirit-filled believers can have joy.
      1. Phil. 4:11
      2. Acts 16:25—Paul and Silas still had joy even in prison.
      3. We should have joy and happiness in our homes.
      4. We need to show and express that joy in our homes.

II. **Spirit-Filled Christians Are Thankful (v. 20)**
   A. Someone defined the home as "the place where we are treated the best . . . and complain the most!"

1. According to marriage counselors, taking each other for granted is one of the chief causes of marital problems.
2. The devil moves in when we complain and criticize.
3. Giving thanks defeats the devil, glorifies God, and draws your heart closer to home.
4. Being thankful for each other is a secret of a happy home.

B. The Holy Spirit is the One who gives us the grace of thanksgiving.
1. We are to be thankful at all times and for all things.
2. Whenever we find ourselves in difficult situations, we should immediately give thanks to the Father in the name of Jesus Christ by the power of the Holy Spirit.
3. 1 Thess. 5:18

III. Spirit-Filled Homes Are Submissive (vv. 21-23)
A. Authority has become an unpopular word.
1. Submission to authority is distasteful to many people.
2. This attitude has permeated even the church.

B. When Paul wrote in verse 21: "Submit to one another out of reverence for Christ," he outlined a principle of major proportion that must be understood in the Christian home.
1. Submitting to Christ.
2. Submitting to one another.
   a. Put others first.
   b. Think about their feelings, desires, and wishes.
   c. Keep minor things minor.
   d. Be flexible.

Conclusion
The hope for our homes is the presence and power of the Holy Spirit living in each and every one of us. When the Holy Spirit takes control, He gives us a joyful, thankful, and submissive heart.

Guidelines for Spirit-Filled Homes—Part 2

Ephesians 5:18-33

Introduction

In Paul's day marriage had fallen short of the ideal. To the Jews who had a very low view of women, a man could divorce his wife for spoiling his dinner, walking in public with her head uncovered, or speaking disrespectfully about his parents. A man could even divorce his wife if he found another woman who looked more attractive. Greek wives were to run the home and care for their husband's legitimate children, but the husband found his pleasure and companionship elsewhere. In Roman culture, the marriage bond was on the way to a complete breakdown. It was not unheard of for a man to be marrying his 23rd wife, and he might be her 21st husband.

Against this background, Paul calls us to a new purity and a new fellowship in the marriage relationship. In verses 23-24, Paul speaks to wives. In verses 25-31, he speaks to husbands.

I. **Wives—Submit (vv. 23-24)**
   A. The motive of submission (v. 23).
      1. Wives are to submit to their husbands as they submit to the Lord.
      2. The relationship of the wives to the Lord is one of complete, entire, absolute surrender and submission.
      3. They are to submit to their husbands out of their love and reverence for the Lord.
      4. Their submission is an expression of their salvation to the Lord.
         a. They are not submitting for the husband.
         b. They are submitting for the sake of the Lord.
   B. The reason of submission (v. 23).
      1. This is part of God's creation, His will and decree (Gen. 3:16; 1 Pet. 3:7).
      2. Man is to be the head of the wife and head of the home.
      3. Woman was created to be a complement, a helpmate, and a support of man.

C. The relationship of the Church to Christ (vv. 23-24). Paul uses the example of the Church's devotion to Christ as a wife's devotion for her husband.

II. Husbands—Love (vv. 25-31)

Sometimes the emphasis of this passage is entirely misplaced. The basis of the passage is not one of control; it is one of divine love. Paul describes the love that a husband should have for his wife.

A. Husbands, love your wives with a sacrificial love (v. 25).
 1. We are to love our wives as Christ loved the Church.
  a. A love that is undying in devotion.
  b. A love that is sensitive to her needs.
  c. A love that is self-denying in attention.
 2. Christ willingly laid down His life for the Church.
B. Husbands, love your wives with a sanctifying love (vv. 26-27).
 1. Sanctifying love empowers the wife to fulfill the plan God has for her.
 2. Sanctifying love enriches the wife and cherishes her as a treasure.
 3. Sanctifying love cleanses the relationship and removes anything that would be detrimental to their relationship.
C. Husbands, love your wives with a satisfying love (vv. 28-31).
 1. Husbands are to treat their wives as part of their own bodies.
 2. Husbands are to love and care for their wives.
 3. Husbands are to nourish and cherish their wives.

Conclusion

Marriage is a beautiful gift from God. God wants us to have heaven in our homes and in our marriage relationships. We can have it! Wives, submit to your husbands as to the Lord. Husbands, love your wives as Christ loved the Church with a sacrificial, sanctifying, satisfying love. Husbands and wives, submit to the Holy Spirit, and He will work miracles in your homes.

Guidelines for Spirit-Filled Homes—Part 3

Ephesians 6:1-4

Introduction
Conscientious parents recognize how difficult it is to exercise their God-given authority over their children. There is a delicate balance of being tough, yet tender. Some parents intensify a rebellious spirit by being dictatorial and harsh, while others yield when their authority is tested.

When a strong-willed child resists a parent's authority, the pressure is to give in for the sake of peace and harmony. I am reminded of a frustrated mother who could no longer handle the hassle of constantly saying no to her young son. She finally flung up her hands and shouted, "All right, Billy, do whatever you want! Now let me see you disobey that!"

It is not easy to exercise authority over children. However, early in life children must be taught that God has given their parents the right of authority.

We need fathers and mothers who are strong enough to say no and stick by it, but who also look for every opportunity to say yes. Paul reminds us of the children's responsibility to obey and the parents' responsibility to discipline.

I. Children—Obey
   A. Obedience is right (v. 1).
      1. Obey, listen, pay attention, and submit to your parents.
      2. Obey in the Lord.
         a. Children are to obey, respect, and honor their parents because it is part of their obedience to the Lord.
         b. Children show their love for Jesus by obeying their parents. This is becoming, right, and befitting Christian children.
   B. Obedience is commanded (v. 2).
      1. Honor means showing respect, reverence, and love.
      2. Honor means caring.
      3. God's commandment (Exod. 20:12; Deut. 5:16).

    C. Obedience is blessed (v. 3).
        1. This is a commandment with a promise.
        2. Children who honor their parents can expect spiritual prosperity and long life.

II. Parents—Encourage (v. 4)
    A. Encourage your children.
        1. Don't discourage, exasperate, or provoke.
        2. Encouragement will do more than rebuke will ever do.
    B. Train your children.
        1. This is training by actions.
        2. Bring them up by discipline.
            a. Must discipline in love, not in anger or you might injure their bodies and/or their spirits.
            b. Must be consistent.
            c. Must be fair and reasonable.
            d. Must not humiliate them.
            e. Must be exercised in *love!*
    C. Instruct your children.
        1. This is training by words.
        2. Obligation to prepare our children for the things that are wrong. Prepare them for temptation, trials, and tricks of the devil.
        3. Obligation to train our children in the things of God.
        4. A great need of our day is for parents to bring their children up in the discipline and admonition of the Lord.

Conclusion

    The most important training ground for the education and discipline of your children is a Christian home where Mom is submitted to Dad. A home where Dad loves Mom as Christ loved the Church, a home where parents encourage, discipline, and instruct their children in the things of the Lord. The only way to have that kind of home is for the home to be filled with the Holy Spirit.

Is There Hope for the Family?

Ephesians 5:33

Introduction
The American family is in crisis! Many say it is disintegrating and its survival is hopeless. Considering that:
 One out of every two marriages end in divorce.
 Seventy percent of schoolchildren come from divorced homes.
 The leading cause of death among children is no longer measles, mumps, cancer, but homicide.
 Two million children are abused each year.
 The average family spends only 14 minutes a day talking to their children and 12 of those minutes the parents are telling them what to do and what not to do.
 A recent study at Cornell University found that the average father spends 37.7 seconds a day with his children and yet the average child spends four hours a day watching television.
 Is there hope for the family? Is there hope for your family and your marriage?

I. **The Confusion**
   A. I am confused why in so many marriages and families the old saying is true: "Familiarity breeds contempt."
   B. Why is it that we treat strangers nicer that we treat our own family?
   C. Why is it that even though we are Christians our marriages and family lives are still in trouble?

II. **The Clarification**
   A. I think I know why; let me explain through an illustration. Yesterday I was mowing my lawn; I couldn't believe the weeds and the bare spots. I started looking at my neighbors' yards and how they were. My wife came out and I complained and she said, "Go look at their yards up close." I walked over to their yard and they had bare spots and weeds too.

    B. We live so close to our own families that we see all the bare spots and the weeds.
       1. We look at the supposedly greener grass on the other side of the fence and we say, "Oh, that is so much better than what I have."
       2. And we become discontented with what we have, we start taking it for granted, we lose respect for it.
       3. We think that our wife, husband, children are not perfect. (They probably are not perfect).
          a. Husband, your wife may not be perfect.
          b. Wife, your husband may not be perfect.
          c. Parents, your children may not be perfect.
          d. Children, your parents may not be perfect.
          e. But neither is anyone else!

III. The Biblical Consideration

    A. Paul tells us we are to respect and love one another. We are to give attention, special consideration, high regard, esteem, and honor to one another.
    B. Respect one another in our thoughts. Open our minds and eyes to think and see the positive instead of the negative, the good instead of the bad, the strengths instead of the weaknesses (Phil. 3:8).
    C. Respect one another in our actions.
       1. Consideration
       2. Communication
       3. Compassion

Conclusion

Is there hope for our homes? Yes, if we start working on our relationships with our spouses and children. Yes, if we give our spouses and children the consideration, the communication, and the compassion they need. There is hope for the home! There is hope for your home!

Ready for Battle—Part 1

Ephesians 6:10-24

Introduction
Paul wrote this masterpiece of Christian literature while chained to a Roman soldier (6:20). Night and day a soldier was there to ensure that Paul would not escape. During his imprisonment he had seen many Roman soldiers and had observed their dress, weapons, and preparation for battle. In verses 10-24 Paul compares the soldier's armor to the Christian life. Part by part Paul takes the armor of the Roman soldier and translates it into Christian terms. In these verses Paul helps us understand three truths that enable us to stand in victory.

I. **Our Adversary (vv. 10-12)**
   A. Our enemy is the devil, the slanderous accuser, the great adversary, and the fierce foe of the Christian.
      1. We are not battling against mere human beings.
      2. Our battle is against Satan and his forces.
   B. Satan is strong.
      1. He is a powerful and formidable enemy.
      2. To stand against him, we must have the power of God (1 Pet. 5:8; John 10:10).
   C. Satan is subtle (v. 11). He is wise and we must fight against his schemes, craftiness, and strategies (2 Cor. 11:3; 12:7).
   D. Satan represents a struggle (v. 12).
      1. Paul switches from a picture of a soldier in armor to a wrestler stripped for action.
      2. We are not mere spectators of a game.
      3. We are participants involved in hand-to-hand combat.
   E. Even though Satan and his forces are formidable, greater is he that is with us than he that is against us.
      1. Satan is no match for the Lord.
      2. Through the Lord we can be more than conquerors.
      3. We can be victorious over our adversary.
      4. We have been given armor to equip us for the battle.

II. Our Armor (vv. 13-17)
A. The belt of truth (v. 14)
1. The belt served two purposes:
    a. When soldiers were about to enter battle, they tucked the tunic up under the belt in order to have their legs free for battle.
    b. The belt served as a place to fasten the breastplate and hold the sword.
2. What does it mean to fasten the belt of truth?
    a. Jesus said, "I am the way, the truth, and the life" (John 14:6).
    b. Jesus is not just one way but the *only* way.
    c. Jesus is not just a part of the truth, but He is ultimate truth.
    d. Jesus is not just an option to life, but He is the key to life.
    e. He is all you need to find joy, happiness, and peace.
3. When Satan comes and tells us we need something more than Jesus to find joy, happiness, and peace, we can tell him to take a hike. Jesus is all we need.
4. He has brought forgiveness, freedom, peace of heart and mind, contentment, and a future in heaven.
5. Tighten the belt of truth.
B. The breastplate of righteousness (v. 14)
1. The breastplate symbolizes the believer's righteousness "in Christ."
2. Christ is the ground for our righteousness standing before God (2 Cor. 5:21; 1 Cor. 1:30; Phil. 3:9).
3. The devil attacks many believers at their emotions and their feeling of unworthiness.
    a. He brings up past sins.
    b. He makes us feel unworthy.
    c. He robs us of our assurance.
    d. He loads us down with guilt for the past.
4. How do we answer Satan's attacks?
    a. Don't stand on your own merit.
    b. Our righteousness is as filthy rags before God.
    c. We come on the merit of Jesus, on the grounds of His righteousness imparted to us (1 Cor. 15:9-10; Rom. 8:1).

C. The shoes of the gospel of peace
      1. It is our peace with Christ that enables us to stand firmly in the slippery places and during the difficult times of our lives.
      2. Jesus Christ is our peace, calm, and courage (Eph. 2:14; Rom. 5:1; Phil. 4:7).
      3. Our peace with God and our peace with others enable us to stand firmly (James 3:14, 17-18; Heb. 12:14; Eph. 4:3).

Conclusion

We are in a spiritual battle against a strong adversary. However, we have been given spiritual armor to protect us in the battle, so we can be victorious. Here's the challenge—put on the armor: the belt of truth around our waist, the breastplate of righteousness guarding our hearts, and the shoes of the gospel of peace to help us stand firmly. All these are found in Jesus. Jesus is all we need.

> *All that I need, He will always be,*
> *All that I need till His face I see,*
> *All that I need till eternity,*
> *Jesus is all I need.*

Ready for Battle–Part 2

Ephesians 6:10-24

Introduction
Each morning we make preparation for a new day. Some people prepare the night before by thinking about what they will wear the next day. Some even lay out their clothes. In these verses the apostle Paul is telling us to get prepared spiritually by putting on the armor of God. To Paul, the Christian life is not a playground, but a battlefield.

I. Our Armor (vv. 13-17)

We have considered the belt of truth, the breastplate of righteousness, and the shoes of the gospel of peace. Let us next look at:

A. The shield of faith (v. 16)
  1. Satan shoots "fiery darts" at our hearts and minds.
     a. Sometimes they come as evil thoughts.
     b. Sometimes they come flooding in as doubt.
     c. Sometimes they come as fear and anxieties.
  2. How do we counteract or extinguish these fiery darts?
     a. We must take up the shield of faith (v. 16).
     b. It is not just saving faith, but a living faith.
     c. It is acting upon what we believe.
     d. It is acting upon the facts of our faith and not just our feelings.

B. The helmet of salvation (v. 17)
  1. Satan wants to attack our emotions and also our minds.
     a. He defeated Eve (Gen. 3; 2 Cor. 11:3).
     b. Our minds play an important and vital role in our Christian growth, service, and victory.
     c. We must guard our minds from the polluting influences of our world (Phil. 4:7-9; Col. 3:2).
  2. God wants to control our minds so that Satan cannot lead us astray.
  3. We have a hope of salvation (1 Thess. 5:8).
     a. Forgiveness for past sins.

    b. Deliverance in the present.
    c. Victory for the future.
  C. The sword of the Spirit (v. 17)
    1. The Word of God is sharp and is able to pierce and penetrate the inner person.
    2. The Word of God is our only offensive weapon.
    3. God's Word is indispensable.
    4. Jesus used the sword of the Spirit in His temptations (Luke 4:1-13).
    5. God's Word is valuable to us in our spiritual battles.
      a. God's Word exposes the sinfulness of our actions and thoughts.
      b. God's Word gives us God's viewpoint and perspective.
      c. God's Word helps displace sinful thoughts.
      d. God's Word releases faith.
    6. We must become familiar with our weapon, the Word of God. "Let the Word of Christ dwell in you richly" (Col. 3:16; see Ps. 119:9-16).

Conclusion

  God has protection for you for the spiritual battles you face. He has graciously given you the equipment you need to be victorious. Be sure every day you have on the full armor of God so you can stand strong against Satan's attacks. Put on the belt of truth, the breastplate of righteousness, the shoes of the gospel of peace, and take up the shield of faith. Put on the helmet of salvation, and take up the sword of the Spirit, which is the Word of God. You can be more than a conqueror through Christ who strengthens you.

Our Advantage in Battle—Prayer

Ephesians 6:10-24

Introduction
In the battle against Satan and the forces of evil, believers have been given spiritual armor. True believers not only stand their ground but also are given a powerful advantage through the offensive weapons of the Word of God and prayer. Consider the formidable weapon we have in faith as we communicate with the Commander-in-Chief.

I. **We Must Have Divine Energy to Stand Fast in the Battles of Life**
   A. We can have the best armor and still be of no help in the battle unless we have the energy we need.
   B. We have been given a divine lifeline through prayer.

II. **The Potential of Prayer Is Staggering**
   A. Prayer is the energy that enables us to wear the armor and use the sword.
   B. S. D. Gordon wrote, "Prayer is striking the winning blow, service is gathering up the results."
   C. E. M. Bounds wrote, "God shapes the world by prayer. God conditions the very life and prosperity of His cause on prayer."
   D. Prayer should be the main business of our day.
   E. Through the channel of prayer we find power for victory.

III. **The Problem of Prayer Is Self (Gal. 5:16-18)**
   A. We can walk in the flesh or in the Spirit.
   B. The flesh has no desire to pray.
   C. I believe that prayerlessness is not primarily a lack of discipline, a lack of opportunity, or a lack of time; it is primarily a problem of trying to pray in the flesh.

IV. **The Provision of Prayer Is the Spirit**
   A. The Holy Spirit has been given to enable us to pray.

B. It is not by might nor by power, but by His Spirit (see Zech. 4:6; Rom. 8:26-27).

V. The Possibilities of Prayer Are Stimulating
A. The possibility of unbroken fellowship with God.
B. The possibility of confidence, communion, and conformity to His image.
C. The possibility of intercession for others.

Conclusion

You are in a battle! It is a battle you can win! You must put on the full armor of God, so you can stand strong against Satan's attacks. Stand with the advantage of prayer. Through prayer God will energize you to win the battles and keep the victory. You can be more than a conqueror through Christ who gives you strength!